Speed's War

Speed's War

A CANADIAN SOLDIER'S MEMOIR
OF WORLD WAR II

By George A. Reid

Madrona Books & Publishing

Cover photographs from the collection of the author.

Published by
Madrona Books & Publishing
3909 Marine Drive, Royston, B.C.   V0R 2V0

Editor: Margaret Cadwaladr
Copy Editor: Judith Brand
Design: John McKercher

LIBRARY AND ARCHIVES CANADA CATALOGUING IN PUBLICATION

Reid, George A. (George Alexander), 1923–
Speed's war: a Canadian soldier's memoir of World War II/by
George A. Reid.

Includes index.
ISBN 978-0-9730096-2-0

1. Reid, George A. (George Alexander), 1923– 2. World War,
1939–1945—Prisoners and prisons, German. 3. Prisoners of war
—Germany—Biography. 4. World War, 1939–1945—Personal
narratives, Canadian. I. Title.

D811.R43 2007   940.54'72'092   C2007-902586-2

Printed in Canada on recycled paper
by Transcontinental Printing.

To the guys

who were in the salt mines

with me.

DISCARD

Contents

Acknowledgments

Many people played a role in creating this book. Margaret Cadwaladr extracted my story from many pages of handwritten notes and recollections. She also transcribed and edited the material. Several people read the draft that resulted and made helpful comments on it. They include Sharon Lockhart, Jim McLardy, John England, Jim Cadwaladr, Dr. John Coady, Norm Christie and Mark Zuehlke. John McKercher designed the book, and Judith Brand copyedited it. I would like to thank each of them. Above all, I want to thank my wife, Paula. I married Paula in June 1947, and I am grateful to her for putting up with me for all these years.

Author's Note

I don't mean to try to make a hero of myself in this short narrative of my experiences while in Sicily, Italy and eight POW camps. Many men did much more and gave much more. A lot would not have the thrill of coming home to family and friends, and seeing the changes in the hometown and country and the world that they fought and died for. This is not a thriller or a tall tale. This is a record of my own experiences during World War II. I recorded these memories several years after the end of the war and reconstructed dialogue as accurately as possible. Although some names and details are hazy, I recall the events vividly.

1

Joining Up

It was the Great Depression, and like many boys, I dropped out of high school when I was only fourteen years old. Work was scarce, and I was helping to support my family by working at Burrard Dry Dock in North Vancouver, British Columbia. The boys and men looking for work would walk to the gate of the shipyard each morning. We would hang around until nine or ten then go home. Once you got onto a riveting gang, which I eventually did, you would know that if the gang went to work, you did too. I was lucky enough to get on with one of the top gangs, and if the lead hand found out he had a job to do, he would phone me.

When we did work, we would work two or three shifts. Once a job came in, it was usually rush, rush, rush. Ships would run aground in a fog and had to be quickly back out on the run, especially if it was one of the coastal freighters or a passenger ship. The Union and CPR ships all helped to keep Burrard Dry Dock going. I remember dragging myself fifteen blocks home dead tired after some of these twenty-four-hour shifts. On payday, I would give my mother my pay envelope, she would give me fifty cents to spend, and that was grudgingly given.

Later, when war was declared I worked steady and got five dollars a week until I went to Pacific Dry Dock and started steel caulking. Then I made ninety-five cents an hour, then seven dollars and twenty cents a day, seven days a week. This was good money, and sometimes we would work overtime to clean up a job. My allowance from my mom rose to five dollars.

I had to wait until I was old enough to join the military. I would have joined up right away when war was declared, but my mother said I would have to stay in Canada, as I was underage. So, we made a deal. If the Americans got into the war before I was nineteen I could go. On December 7, 1941, the Japanese bombed Pearl Harbor, and it was time. I thought I would have a last Christmas with my family, and in January 1942, two weeks before my nineteenth birthday, I joined up.

I tried to join the navy first, but the recruiting officer was out to lunch. I said:

"Well, that's his tough luck." I joined the army instead. I initially joined the Canadian Scottish and later transferred to the Seaforth Highlanders.

After enlisting, I spent time around the old

Vancouver Hotel for a couple of weeks and went home each night to North Vancouver. Then we were off to Vernon for basic training. Training was quite vigorous. They tried to prepare us for battle by making the training as realistic as possible. When they shot over our heads with machine guns, we had to dive for cover. On each dive, I thought I would land on a rattlesnake. But it never happened. The food was okay.

After our basic training, we were given a week's leave. We went home, and then we were off to Calgary for more training at the Currie Barracks. There we trudged around in the muddy clay gumbo. It built up the legs because each foot had ten to twenty pounds of gumbo on it. When you could finally kick the mud off, those army boots felt like slippers.

When we finished our advanced training, we had a short embarkation leave. I went home and said my goodbyes to the folks and my friends. Some came to see me off as we were loaded onto the trains. I don't know where the railroad got the old cars, but I am sure they were old when they were used for World War I and this was twenty years later. It took us five days to cross Canada to the ships waiting in Halifax. We left the next day.

We landed up the Clyde River at Greenoch, had to come ashore in "lighters," and then marched to the trains that would take us to southern England.

That trip to the south was just like in the movies and in newsreels. Another troop train and all of us waving out the windows. I think they figured it helped the morale of the British to see more troops coming. Some of us went to Camp Whitley, a holding unit. We would stay there until the Seaforths needed someone.

I decided to take a drivers course to fill in the time. I figured it would be handy to have a second option to fall back on. As it happened, I was sent to the battalion as a driver. So I spent a lot of the year in England driving a truck. Driving in convoy at night was tricky. It kept you on your toes. You had to follow a tail light one-quarter of an inch across. If you lost it, you were in trouble. You had to catch up, but not too fast or you could run into the driver in front.

After a while I was shipped back to my outfit. I reported to the transport platoon, which was in a World War I airport hanger on the south coast. Here I saw my first action. I was in the back of the hanger, and we heard explosions. The air-raid siren went off, and anti-aircraft guns were firing. A German airplane flew past the door. It was only thirty or forty feet off the ground. The ack ack gun got it a mile or so away. We jumped into a couple of trucks and went to where he had dropped the bombs and helped to dig out the wounded and dead. One bomb had hit a pub downtown.

I left the transport unit and went into D Company, a rifle company. We did our training in Inveraray at the commando training area, then at Hamilton Race Course just out of Glasgow. From there, I could visit my relatives on my dad's side of the family. One day, they issued us summer drill or tropical gear, and the rumours started. The betting was we were going to Norway. The gear was just to throw Jerry's spies off-track. Soon we were loaded on the *Circassia* moored in the Clyde River at Greenoch, the same place we landed when we came from Canada. I had been in Britain for a year.

We sat on the ship for days before we sailed. Once we even landed on the other side of the river and went on a march for exercise. When we did sail, we headed west, then east, then west, then east in a big circle. Then the convoy from North America joined us. Later they said it was the largest armada ever to be assembled.

Our ship was third from the front and on the left side. The black flag was raised several times to warn of a submarine. We were supposed to go below, but I thought it was stupid to put 5,000 men below to die if we were torpedoed, so I would stay on deck. One day the flag was raised, and a navy ship cut across our bow. Another two came in from the horizon on our port side. The ship up front laid a pattern of depth charges, stopped and turned around. The ship that cut across our bow laid another pattern and turned sharply. A steel plate flew into the air, and soon the tail of a submarine came out of the water, and with a hiss of air, it went straight down. A loud cheer went up all over the convoy, but I couldn't help thinking of the poor devils on the sub and the panic and desperation they must have felt. I couldn't help but feel sorry for them.

We went through Gibraltar at night. When we entered the Mediterranean, it was strange to see streetlights and car lights moving along the shore after the blackouts in England. I was sitting in my favourite place, on top of one of the makeshift toilets built on each side of the forward hatch. Soon a storm blew up. Although our ship was a fair size, the waves were coming over the bow. They became so large they splashed over my private deck, so I had to vacate to higher ground. We watched the LSTs (Landing Ship Tanks) and LSIs (Landing Ship Infantry) that joined us from North Africa. They would go out of sight for minutes at a time, and we thought they had gone, but they popped back up. It must have been hell for them because they had flat bottoms for landing on the beach and had not been built for those kinds of seas.

2

Sicily

WE WERE TO LAND on Sicily at 2 A.M. on the July 10, 1943, as part of Montgomery's 8th Army. The invasion of Sicily was probably very simple to the Chiefs of Staff sitting in London, but to the guys about to be killed or wounded, it was not. It was scary. Everyone was sweating. The word was they would beach the mother ships if the weather didn't let up, but land we did. Fortunately, the storm was abating. I looked around me in the landing barge and thought, "It's just like a movie, only I'm in it." We were third in line, and the ships went back as far as the eye could see.

The operator of our craft ran us up and down the beach until we told him to either land the god-damned boat or we would land it for him. Now, you have to realize we certainly did have the equip-ment to use force against this guy or to mutiny. So he turned towards Sicily as if he had just found our beach; Amber was the code name. Don't get me

wrong, the navy did a fantastic job, but this guy...
Well, it's too long a story.

I'll never forget climbing down the rope nets
to the landing craft. The ramp went down, and we
walked into water five-feet deep. Smokey Smith
was in front of me, although he was supposed to
be behind me. Well, we hit the water, and Smokey
was going under, so I picked him up by the col-
lar and held him up. I was six to ten inches taller
than Smokey. Thank God I was able to grab him,
because he made a hell of a lot better soldier than I
did; later on, he won the Victoria Cross.

I couldn't get over the feeling of being there,
right in the middle of an invasion. I wondered
what my family thought. I supposed they would be
worried. As for myself, I was wary about what to
expect. I feared this is going to be another damned
fiasco like Dieppe the year before. We'll be pinned
down, and a lot of us will be casualties, I thought.
I knew we had a bank to climb. I felt the enemy
would be counterattacking at any time and that
all hell would break loose. I expect everyone right
up to the colonel thought the same thing. It was
a mixture of excitement and fear, knowing that
you were a part of a historic event. I was a part of
the largest invasion of all time. Of course, D-Day
later on was much larger, but they had only a short
distance to go compared to our journey to Sicily.
I was proud to be there, and I knew we could lick

the Germans and the Italians were not much of a threat.

Things turned out okay. The bank wasn't too bad, and I guess Jerry didn't think anyone would invade in a storm like that. We had little opposition on our front. Only a few rounds were shot off.

The Mediterranean sun beat down on us all day long. Even in shorts, we would just sweat, standing or sitting. I found out later the temperature was about 113° F (45° C). Then came the first of the perpetual orders: "OK. Let's move on." And "OK. Dig in." I am sure the chap that invented the hydraulic backhoe was a soldier in Sicily. That dirt was baked as hard as rock. We could barely scoop out enough to pile around us. The German trench was always deeper and nicer. Some of them were chest deep, but you never knew when they had been booby-trapped with mines.

We marched past farm-houses with brilliant whitewashed walls. The first time we were under fire, I dove to the ground and placed my Bren gun on an object in the garden I happened to be going through. Then I noticed it was a beautiful big watermelon. Then I said to Smokey Smith, my number two, "Boy, a watermelon! What a great war this is going to be." I was just going to break it open when the order came to move on. I never saw another watermelon in Sicily.

We stopped for our first meal and opened tins

of soup. They had a canned heat attachment that I know worked very well because I scalded my mouth with it. That added to problems I didn't need on our first day. From here on, we slept where we stopped in ditches in slit trenches a foot deep. I cursed my six feet, wishing I was shorter so I didn't have to dig the longer slit trench. Our trench tools bounced off the hard-baked ground.

When the tanks and artillery landed, we felt more secure because up until then, we had nothing but our own anti-tank bazookas to fight off a counterattack. The tanks passed us kicking up more dust, then the artillery came up with trucks and cars. As we advanced and I looked about me at the hundreds of men marching in single file and trucks, tanks and artillery, I felt a mixture of excitement, fear and pride.

Our first taste of German pinpoint artillery came a few days after the landing. We had to stop for some reason, and the word came down: "Dig in." We spread out on each side of the road and proceeded to dig. There was an explosion not ten feet behind me, and a corporal in my section was blown to bits. I grabbed my Bren and ran down the hill and got behind a stone wall and fired at the 88 mm, the large German high-velocity gun that had fired at us. The big guns then pulled back because this is what they did: Fire a few shots and move before we could bring artillery or tank fire on them.

It was mostly mortars called Moaning Minnies. Jerry would leave a machine-gun emplacement to hold us up for awhile. These were mostly nuisance tactics to give them time to retreat.

The Italians surrendered in complete units and then volunteered to work for us behind the lines. It was nothing to see a couple of hundred of them walking towards us, hands raised and a white flag. We would tell them to keep walking, and someone in rear would feed them. At first we sent a couple of men back with them, but after a few days, we just said go to a certain place and they would be fed. This worked quite well. I can't blame them as they were in a no-win situation. If they helped the Germans, they knew it was only a matter of time before they lost their own country to Germany.

The supply people must have had their hands full to feed us and the POWs as well. Besides this, they had to bring up ammunition, gas, medical supplies and vehicles, all the things needed to carry on a war.

Soon we would see some evidence of fighting, a truck or tank burned out. The air force or artillery had knocked them out from the rear as we were coming up. The odd Canadian vehicle, perhaps an armoured reconnaissance car, was burned out. This would make you think of the poor guys inside and their folks at home, not knowing yet that their loved one wouldn't be coming home.

The smell of war is something you never forget. You could smell a shot-up convoy or a shelled town long before you got to it. The smell of burnt bodies or just dead bodies, you never forget. Even if the towns or villages weren't bombed or shelled, you could smell them long before you saw them. At first it was the urine. We blamed the donkeys. Later it was the stench of dead and bloated bodies along with the urine from the animals. To this day, when I watch fighting on the television in areas of unrest in the world, the smells come back to me. You smelled a body, then moved closer. You felt a feeling of relief if you saw a German uniform on him. Finally, I would think, he's just like us, he probably didn't want to come here either.

We took the towns of Assoro, Leonforte and Agira. Agira was an interesting place. The German 15th Panzer Grenadier regiment had settled in and made a stand in the mountain village. Once, we watched our tanks zigzagging up the narrow streets and Jerry tanks coming the other way. I ran to our radioman and warned him. He said he would try to get through, and I think he must have because the first Canadian tank stopped just short of the last turn and knocked out a Tiger as it came around the corner. Agira was taken on July 28 after five days of heavy fighting. We were kind of proud of this as the Jerry Panzer outfit was a crack unit and had been through the desert war.

At one point, the Edmonton Regiment was pinned down in Leonforte. We were preparing to help them when the British heavy artillery hit our hill instead of Leonforte. They knocked the hell out of us. Several shells landed in the headquarters area, killing and wounding a lot of men. I dove into my slit trench that was on the edge of a gully. I could cover the trail below with my Bren gun. One shell landed directly below me by five or six feet. It lifted me clear out of my trench and knocked the wind out of me.

After the shelling stopped we picked up the dead and wounded. I helped to give covering fire for a frontal attack so the Edmonton Regiment could get out. Few of the attack company came back unscratched. I said a few words of thanks as I had come awful close to getting blown to pieces.

We sent a volunteer platoon on a frontal attack to draw Jerry's fire, and they sure did. We took a heavy toll in this skirmish. Later that afternoon, a company was made up from the rest of the battalion led by Major Bell-Irving. We crossed in front of Leonforte and up a goat trail to high ground behind the town. We left our platoon commander at the bottom of the trail suffering from battle fatigue. On reaching the top, Bell-Irving fired a flare, signalling our position to battalion HQ. It also signalled our position to several Jerry tanks and armoured cars that raked us with machine-gun fire. I dove into a hollow filled with cactus. The guns sheared them off like a scythe. They either got tired of shooting or ran out of ammunition.

Later that night we faced another foul-up. We were to take up positions in the rear, and as the artillery shelled, we were to catch Jerry coming out the back. Jerry opened up on us with machine guns from his armour. I ran out and found fifteen guys trying to decide what to do. There was a corporal with them, and the rest had no fighting experience. The corporal asked if I would take charge, as he was a clerk at HQ. I did know what the object was, so I said, "OK" and told them what I knew. Well, we started to carry out our objective—take the cut down the road and get Jerry when they retreated through it. We walked down through a nut orchard and I spotted the cut, but on the way, I heard a machine gun being cocked, so I ran to the base of the hill and shouted: "Come on. Let's get them."

When I looked around, I was by myself. About then, Jerry threw a potato masher on my left side. It rolled me over a couple of times. Then one landed on my right. It rolled me back. Then another on my left. When I stopped rolling, I ran a burst along the top edge of the hill. Someone let out a yell, and I ran for the first tree. I let them have another burst, heard a scream and ran till I hit the bottom of the hill. While I was running, tracer bullets were all around me and one burned the inside of my arm. I wasn't hurt badly. That's close.

It was warm, and I needed a drink of water; I had given my last bit to a fellow who was hit when the armour shot us up earlier. I met up with a sergeant who I didn't like, but we felt we would stand a better chance together. We found a well, but the water was putrid, so we moved on. Some Jerries spotted us and pinned us down for forty-eight hours.

We finally got out and made it to an orange grove where we found an old man on a bench in the shade of a veranda. He took one look at us, jumped off of his bench, and sat us on it. Then he hurried over to the well and brought us some water. He wouldn't give us much, though. The grapes and oranges in Sicily were good. I don't know if the farmer had any left when we got through with them. But I know one thing: We ate the grapes and we fertilized the ground, so all was not lost.

We rested for an hour and then set out to find the battalion. When we did, they were just moving out. The officer said we were in the books as missing. We fell in and marched. We took a few more towns and villages, and lost more men.

At times we would send out five or six men on a reconnaissance. On one of these, we ran into an area that Jerry had pretty well zeroed in on. He was high up; we were in a valley. He was firing on another target past us. One of the fellows stood out in the open with binoculars, looking at them. The rest of us took cover amongst a bunch of large rocks. Jerry, whether he was fooling around or not, put the first round between that guy's feet. It was either a dud or an amour-piercing shell. It might well have gone off. The soldier just collapsed. We had to carry him back, and he went down the line. We never saw him again.

The rest of Jerry's shells were not duds, however. We thought he was trying to blast the pile of rocks away. We stood and cheered from our vantage point. It was like watching a show. Later that day, a strange thing happened. We had dug in, and in our ever-exhausted state, I fell asleep. When I woke up, I couldn't feel my legs. I thought I must have been hit and lost both my legs. I was scared to look. The Sergeant said:

"You OK, Reid?"

"Are my legs OK?" I asked.

"They look OK to me," he replied.

Then I realised what the problem was. My legs were just numb. Boy was I relieved.

In August, Sicily fell and we went to a place near Militello we came to know as "Happy Valley." There we were able to rest and recuperate. Our resting place was in an irrigated valley filled with olive groves. It was like heaven. It was a nice green spot, a small creek running through. It was a break from the hot Italian sun. We washed in a pool that formed when we built a dam in the creek. I got new boots, and I wore them when I washed in the creek so they dried to the shape of my feet.

3

The Scout Platoon

At one of the reunions, I think it was the fiftieth, one of the old vets asked me what company I was in. I said Headquarters Company and the scout platoon. He looked at me and said, "You must have been crazy."

I told him, "Yep. That helped."

The rest of the battalion thought that we were a little different. We were, and we were damn proud of it. The scout-sniper platoon was a volunteer platoon and consequently was never up to strength. We never had more than two-thirds of a platoon, which meant we had to go out more. The job was to go out equipped with Lee Enfield No. 4 Snipers rifles and find weak spots in the Jerry's lines. We looked around his lines; sometimes we made a nuisance of ourselves and did a little sniping. Then we snuck back and reported to Lieut. Gray. At one time, the whole platoon advanced and ended up behind Jerry's line. We lay and watched his moves all night and the next day.

I don't know when the scout-sniper platoon was started, but it was in Sicily. Sergeant McKee had asked me if I would like to join it. He told me it was a strictly volunteer platoon and if I said no, that would be it. By this time, I thought a change might be good as there was only about four or five of the original platoon left. We got the idea our days were numbered. I told the Sergeant to count me in. I was the first one he asked.

"OK, I'll arrange it with the CO, and you go out and find a horse," he said

"A what?" I said.

"A horse," he said.

He explained that the platoon was going to be mounted. I was no cowboy. I didn't think I could ride well enough to join them.

I said, "Let me know when they got rid of the horses and I'll join you." I had enough trouble digging a big enough hole for me, let alone for a horse.

He asked if I would help round up some horses anyway, and I said sure. I brought in a mule; I didn't know the difference. McKee took it himself and had it and two horses shot out from under him, one of them as he lay behind it. The machine gun nest shot that horse until the gunner was cleaned out.

Later, while we rested in Happy Valley, Sergeant McKee came to me and said: "George, we got rid of the horses. Will you join us now?" I did.

The scout platoon was made up of a great bunch of guys. You could count on them to back you up. It was hard on the nerves, however. We led every advance and went on all the reconnaissance patrols. It was a lot to ask of one platoon that was never up to strength. You never really knew if a sniper was waiting to get a better shot at you or not. There is one thing you knew for sure: You knew when your cover was discovered. If bullets start to snap around you, it was you and not someone else they were shooting at. There wasn't anyone else there.

Like all good things that come to an end, we left Happy Valley and were on the road once more. In early September 1943, we rode on trucks up to Messina where we boarded landing barges to cross the straits of Messina to invade Italy. We travelled up the road to Taranto at the bottom of the boot of Italy. The Germans had left either a lot earlier or by truck because we went for five days and four nights and didn't catch them. We were exhausted. We finally had to stop because our supplies had run out. By this time, we had seen the lights of Taranto, but had turned inland and up toward Bari. Around this area, we had our first torrential rain. That night we billeted in a school, soaked to the skin. Several

Italians came in with accordions and mandolins. It was nice, but I think most of us fell asleep before they finished playing.

Advancing in the Italian mountains was even more nerve-wracking. We walked up steep, dusty gullies. It was like walking up the Fraser Canyon back home in British Columbia, but with nowhere to take cover from enemy fire. The scout platoon always led the way. It was our job to try to spot the rear-action machine guns before they got us. It was tough. Every curve in the road, you expected to be met by a burst of machine guns or an 88 mm cannon, and occasionally we were. Some of the gun nests blended into the rock formation so well they couldn't be spotted until you were right on top of them. Luckily, some of the formations would be impossible to get out of, so Jerry didn't man them all. Thank heavens.

About the second or third of October, the platoon was advancing well ahead of the battalion. We came upon a Canadian anti-aircraft gun crew. They said they were lost; they had taken a wrong turn. They didn't know which way to go and pointed out a bunch of Jerries. They were disappointed when we said we couldn't chase them away for them. We had other orders.

They said: "What if they attack?"

"Won't that gun fire horizontally?" I said to one fellow.

"Sure," he said

"Then do it." I said, "You have more firepower than we do."

Lieutenant Gray pointed out the way back on their map.

The advancing went on, and the nervousness built up. There was no shortage of excitement. Some of the advances were across fields with no cover and Jerry throwing everything at us he could find including a railway gun. I think I could have crawled down the barrel; it was that big. It all reminded me of movies of WWI. You don't know how brave a man is until you put him in a spot like that. Jerry would do his damn best, but we always would advance at walking speed with no cover and take the area.

The patrols kept up, and each time the regiment moved or advanced, the scout platoon led the way. And every pillbox we came to and passed, I would thank God. I was really a believer in the Lord. And the laws of average. I kept telling myself they haven't made the shell or built it yet. The trouble was, I was not as sure as I was at first in Sicily. And my nerves were getting worse.

Later, we were heading into a valley, and we passed through a small town I will always remember. The upper stories of the houses on our left side were full of young women. It was astonishing to see so many good-looking young women in one

22

village in Italy. There were about twenty-five or thirty well-dressed and very, I mean very, attractive girls in their late teens and early twenties waving to us. Now this town didn't even seem to be large enough to have a house that big. We later figured it must have been an R&R camp for Jerry. Everyone else lined up along the side of the road. The elderly ladies kissed our hands and gave us bread and eggs. I later read it was a sign of friendliness to offer an egg to someone.

When we reached the other end of town, we each had a helmet full of eggs and a loaf of bread stuck on our bayonet. After the war Lieut. Gray said that when he passed the girls he was afraid to look back in case he didn't have a platoon any longer.

On the way down, one of the scouts explained how to suck an egg by poking a hole at each end. I gagged a bit, but it went down. We were hungry, or I wouldn't have tried it. We also cracked an egg on a helmet and cooked it. It was that hot.

When we reached the valley floor, Brig. Hoff-meister caught up to us in a Jeep. He called Lieut. Gray over for a conference. Lieut. Gray came back smiling. He said Hoffie suggested we stop and cook up some of the eggs and eat the bread so that we would look more like an army ready to fight. We didn't look too smart with helmets full of eggs and a loaf of bread stuck on our bayonet, so we had scrambled, boiled and fried eggs. We took some hard-boiled eggs for later.

Brig. Hoffmeister had come up to see for himself what the hold-up was down the road. The Princess Louise Dragoon Guards (PLDG) ran into some mines and were under fire from a Panzer 88. A PLDG light-armoured reconnaissance support was shot up down the road. We were asked to find the 88, and we split into pairs and fanned out. Our job then was to pick off the crew. Sometimes it would only take one or two shots and they would run, but if they decided to fight, they had a lot of firepower. They usually had two machine guns to protect the gun. So, if you planned to shoot it out with them, you had better have good coverage.

Further down the road an armoured car had hit a mine going around a blown bridge. The Germans had this area covered with an 88, so we were asked to find it. Blackie Blackstop and I paired up. As it happened, the 88 was in the section we were in. We had a conference and decided Blackie had two handguns, and Blackie had a rifle. I had a Bren gun I had picked up earlier from a chap in the field who had no further use for it. I thought it might be useful one day. Being an old Bren gunner, I liked to have all the firepower on some of the reconnaissance we went on.

Blackie and I decided we had Jerry outnumbered eighty-nine to eighty-eight. We decided to go get him. We were getting our positions set up when we heard the self-propelled 88 start up and leave. "I guess they saw us and got scared," we laughed. Actually we were really quite relieved, but we could at least report the 88 had gone. Blackie went back to report and I stayed to look around for more hold-ups.

Most of the rear-guard action was this type of thing. A few shots and pull out. We ran into a bee's nest a couple of days later. They threw everything they had at us: machine guns, snipers, 88s, howitzers and even a railway gun. They caught us advancing over a large field, a farm I guess. It looked like it might be grazing ground. There was a slope up to where they had dug in.

Two or three days later we ran into him again with a lot more of his friends. The support battalion was brought up and set up several Vickers .303 machine guns. They warned us not to move left or right. We could see why. To hit the ridge that Jerry was on, they had to shoot so close to the ground that they cut the grass to a couple of inches. We had taken cover behind several piles of rock to shoot back. These machine guns were clipping the grass between us. It was an uncomfortable feeling with Jerry shooting from the front and our guns from the back.

We sure lost a lot of good men taking that hill. I saw a man get up from the ground. He had been hit while I watched. He was hit again and went down. He tried to get up and fell. I signalled for the Vickers to stop and ran over to him. I put my right arm around him, and my hand went into a hole on his right side. I could feel his broken ribs. He was trying to support his left arm that was just attached by a bit of flesh and skin. Between us, we held it. He had also been hit in the mouth and lost a bunch of teeth. I got him back to a field dressing spot just behind us and later talked to a fellow that took him to a field hospital in one of the Jeep ambulances. He said they figured he would be OK.

Later that night when we searched for wounded and dead, I found a fellow lying wounded. I called for a stretcher and lifted his head off the dirt. We talked. He said he didn't hurt because he couldn't feel anything. He died in my arms just before the stretcher-bearers got to him. We found the wound in his back. The hole was no bigger than the one in my left calf, but God knows how deep it was.

One day we came across a truck that must have belonged to the German signals. There was a set of binoculars about fourteen inches long by eight or nine inches deep. You could see forever with them. I got a hold of them and carried them on a pack board. The binoculars, I used quite frequently. I was looking through them one day when Blackie and I were out on a reconnaissance. The Jerries spotted us and brought an 88 mm down on us. I watched the gunner swing the gun around and then raised it up. That is when I realised he was aiming at us. I yelled to Blackie to run. We managed to get into the forest so Jerry only got one shot off. I was the only one that got hit—a piece of shrapnel pinned my calf muscle. I hobbled up to battalion area and borrowed some pliers off a friend in transport and pulled it out. I was surprised at the length. It was about two-and-a-half or three inches long, so I went and had a patch put on by the Medical Officer. He shot some stuff in the hole and bandaged it.

A ground mist fell early in the evening, making it eerie. Some of us got onto the road. As we walked up it, we heard a motor idling up ahead. Then we saw a shadow of a tank. A Jerry called out: "Was ist das?" We all dove over the bank as they opened up, missing me again. They had a lot of chances that day.

We got back to HQ area to hear we had to send a patrol out to investigate some fires up ahead. Two of us went to investigate. We walked up a road and walked in some tracks, dodging mines. We went about two miles when we found the problem: three or four armoured cars, a Bren gun carrier and a motorcycle. Some had caught fire, some hadn't. There were three or four dead. We looked around for wounded, but found none. So, Jerry had taken the rest prisoner. I'm quite sure a Canadian got away. We saw the tracks of a Bren carrier turn off the road and zigzag through the fields, and we could see where Jerry had been chasing them with a mortar or artillery.

We did find a fender box full of V cigarettes. As we had run out of cigarettes in the platoon, I packed them back on a pack board. They were made in India. They weren't up to much as a good smoke, but better than nothing, and they were welcomed when we got back.

By now I had not slept for 48 hours. It was not long before we reached Baranello. In fact, it could have been the next day. I'm not sure.

4

Capture

THE RUMOUR WAS we would have a ten-day rest near Baranello. We were all tired, and I was shaky and feverish. Early in the morning Lieut. Gray was called for an O group session to discuss plans and tactics for the next movements. I felt kind of sick. I felt chills and I was sweaty. I told a couple of the guys. They said it sounds like malaria, which had been almost epidemic since we landed in Sicily. When Lieut. Gray returned, he asked for three men for a patrol. We were to bring in a prisoner, or proof of his regiment. I said I would go. The sergeant and another man also volunteered. This was going to be the last patrol, and we would get our ten-day rest at last. I figured if I could get this last one in, I would be able to get over the malaria. I found out it took twice that long and then some as it recurs for months or even years.

We left on the patrol, but before we reached the town, we saw a motorcycle on the side of the road. The dispatch rider had crawled into the ditch for cover but was dead. He hadn't been dead too long because he didn't smell too bad. The sergeant unhooked the web belt on the body and slipped the revolver, a 38 I think, and holster off and put them on his own belt. I remember how gentle he was. He pulled the gun out and looked at it, checked the rounds in it as we walked. "Well, he doesn't need it now and another piece of firepower might come in handy," he said. I added that I hoped we wouldn't need too much firepower.

A few yards further, I spotted what I thought was an apple tree, but it turned out to be a pomegranate tree. I thought I'd get some on the way back.

We carried on to the town where we found Captain Newsom of C Company. They had spotted a man in a white coat or smock and figured he was a spotter for the German artillery. They usually wore white duster coats so the artillery could see them. You knew you were in for a barrage if you spotted one. The Captain asked if we could hit him. The sergeant said we could and pointed to me. The man was quite a distance. We estimated how far, and I sat on the floor with my rifle on the windowsill and set my sights. I figured I had a bead on him. I was just about to squeeze a round when Captain Newsom said: "Hold it. I don't think you better, in case he's a civilian." I'll bet he wished he hadn't stopped me because the Germans did shell the town and C Company pulled out.

The third man with us was sent back with a message while Sergeant McKee and I went looking for a German. In retrospect, I don't know why we didn't go after the fellow in the white coat. We looked for a German to take back but couldn't find one. I remember passing a brickyard and thinking that Jerry should have dug in there. It was a natural fort. We climbed a hill to a house that we felt would be a good observation point. Still no Germans, so we hiked back in a big circle.

On the way back we came across a stone house. We knocked on the door after observing it for a while. An old fellow answered the door and asked us in. We went in and sat at the table. There was a long board on the table piled high with spaghetti. The chap said something to a little old lady in a black dress. She went into the pantry and brought out a couple of plates and forks, which she gave to him. He in turn gave them to us. He apologized for not thinking about our different customs. Apparently they just ate from the board. Anyway, the spaghetti was good, and if I had known it was my last meal for so long, I would have eaten more.

Well, we left the house and headed for the Biferno River. If we were to catch a Jerry we would have to cross it. We reached it in half an hour and then skirted it to find a place to wade across. The shallow part was up to our hips. I remember I expected to hear a shot or a machine gun burst any minute, as there was no cover except for the water itself. Anyway, we made it over and back without our prisoner. We were quite disappointed, so we decided to ask some of the Italians what numbers the Germans they'd seen wore on shoulders and what type of uniform. We reached a farmhouse on top of a hill where we had a good vantage point. We sat and chatted with the Italians, and an old woman wanted to stitch the hole in the knee of my pants so I let her. She seemed to feel like she was really doing something. Much later, I thought she would never know what a favour she had done me, as I had to wear those pants for a year and a half.

While the old woman was mending my pants, a boy of ten or so came running up, saying "Tedeschi, Tedeschi". We asked him where? He said there were a lot of Germans heading to Baranello. The Sarg and I figured we better warn the rest of D Company who were in town, so we took off. We hurried across the flat land and up a trail. Just before we reached the first houses, I heard a cough and I called McKee,

"Hold it, Sarg," I said.

But he went right on. Something was wrong. I didn't like it. I smelled cigarette smoke, and it wasn't like ours. It was Turkish tobacco. As it happened, it was dark by the time we got to the edge of town. We kept expecting to be challenged, but nobody was in sight. I'll never forget the feeling of walking into that town supposedly held by us and not seeing a guard. I know I was angry.

"You know, the whole German army could be in here." I said.

"Yea, I don't like it. Let's head for the police department and find out what the hell's going on here," he said.

Sergeant MeKee walked into a building and said it was the police station. But I don't know if it was. There was no one guarding the entrance. We walked in and found quite a few Italians in there. Some were in civvies, so we asked if the Canadian soldiers were still in town. They said yes. We heard that Jerry shelled this town after we left at noon and that a group of people had taken refuge in the building as they thought it was the safest place. Just then there was a knock at the door, and a voice with an English accent called from outside.

"We are pulling out of town. Come out or be left behind."

I opened the door a few inches. I was looking down the barrels of an automatic pistol and a Schmeisser machine gun. I couldn't back up because the Italians were pushing me out of the door. The German officer was pulling my binoculars, and I couldn't make up my mind which had the biggest bore, the pistol or the machine gun. I heard the door slam behind me, and I heard the sergeant empty his revolver at something inside.

By this time, I was out on the street, and the little Kraut was slapping me on the face. In all the movies, they slap with a glove. This guy hadn't seen the movies. His hand was in the glove. I guess like a lot of small men, they like to make the best of a situation if they are holding the winning hand, and this guy was holding the winning hand.

He asked me where the other man was.

"What other man?" I asked

He hit me again. He said there was a sergeant with me when I came into town.

Again I said I was by myself, and I tried to say it loud enough so McKee could hear me. I lied and told him I just came in for some wine. "Do you take me for a fool?" he asked. I didn't really want to answer that, so I lied again and said it was a long time since I was with a girl and I was looking for one. I thought that was stupid enough to be true.

About this time, someone threw a box of Italian hand grenades down on us. I don't know if it was the sergeant or the Italians but these landed all around. The tiny grenades were about the size of lemons and not much more than noisemakers. They were encased in tin, however, and go off on impact, so a couple of Jerries got cut up. That caused a lot of panic. The injured yelled and screamed, and I decided I better leave, so I ran down the street.

I called out the name of the outfit to the sergeant and ran down the cobblestone street. Later I found out that Sergeant McKee was killed that day.

Hobnails and cobblestones are not conducive to fast running, but I do believe I broke the four-minute mile before it was broken in Vancouver in 1954. My nickname wasn't "Speed Reid" for nothing.

Two machine guns started to fire at me. I could see the tracers all around me, and I couldn't understand how I wasn't hit as the tracers are only every fifth bullet. I thought I would never reach the corner. Halfway to where I figured I could turn a corner to get away from the guns, another machine gun cut in from my left. I could not believe they could miss me at such close range. I remember Hoffmeister saying once that Germans are lousy shots. If I got out of there, I'd find him and tell him he was right, I thought.

I think the more scared I got, the faster I ran. I was lifting my feet so high it must have looked funny. I was also trying not to touch the ground, which is impossible, but who thinks of this when you think you are going to get it at any second. I couldn't make the corner with hobnails in my boots and cobblestone streets, but I got out of their line of fire. I ran up a ways and hid behind a small shrub planted in a half barrel. I watched between the barrel and the building and counted nineteen Jerries walk down the street. The twentieth stopped and looked up towards me. I think someone behind me signalled him that I was hiding there. He walked up to where I was lying and said: "Kaputt?"

I lay there playing dead and half expecting a bayonet in the back. But I think he heard or felt my heart pounding. He gave me a kick in the ribs and repeated:

"Kaputt?" I think I must have jumped when he kicked me because he laughed and said

"Ah, nicht kaputt. Komm. Komm. Raus!"

Thank God he was a decent sort of guy. He was a sergeant, so I guess he had seen a bit of action. He marched me down the way the others had gone. I was given two boxes of ammunition to carry. I guess they thought it would slow me down. I knew our boys were on the other side of the road two or three hundred yards away. I hoped they would fire on us so I could make a break.

When we got to the edge of town, we went up a set of stairs, I guess to a headquarters. They questioned why I was in the town and talked to each other. Finally, they told me I was to go with this group and not to try to escape or I would be shot.

It was one of those full moons, as bright as day, and I wished for clouds, but didn't get any. We would stop and they would stand me against a wall. The walls were all whitewashed, and I thought each time, "This is it, they're going to shoot me." I made up my mind. If they looked like they were going to shoot, they had better be quick because I was going to rush them. I kept looking for a way to escape. On the way to the Jerry HQ, we went through a twenty-five-pound barrage from the Canadian army. I hoped I would never have to face our own guns again.

Eventually we reached the town on the other side of the river, and they put me in a stable. It made a good jail because each section had bars on the doors. I finally collapsed there. The malaria had caught up to me. I sweated and shook and shivered for really I don't know how long. I must have lain on that straw for several days. I heard voices in English in the other stalls and realized there were more prisoners being held.

"Anyone there?" they called.

I answered, "Yes. I'm sick. Malaria."

I think the other English-speaking men convinced the guard that I was sick. When the guard came in, they said to get a doctor, but the guard had left. Later, he came to my door and said: "Come." I went with him and another guard who helped me up some stairs. We entered a great big room. It looked like a ballroom. A table was at one end, and an officer was sitting behind the table. I stopped in front of the table and saluted. It caught him by surprise, but he did not return the salute. He asked:

"What is the matter?"

"I'm sick. I have malaria," I said.

He yelled at the guards to take me away. They grabbed me by the arms and helped me back to my stall. Perhaps he figured it was contagious. I don't know how long it was before they came and got me. They took me in a motorcycle with a sidecar. When I saw what they intended to transport me in, I hoped the German was going to take me all the way to the hospital. I planned to jump him and make my way back to the battalion on the bike with him as my prisoner. But soon we stopped, and I was put into an ambulance. So much for the escape plan.

I don't know how long we drove as I slept and shivered. We drove through a town that the Canadian twenty-five-pounders had pulverized. The air force must have helped, as it was nothing but rubble.

I was on the bottom right-hand side of nine men, three rows of three. The trip was very hazy. I didn't care what was happening. Finally, we stopped. I found out later we were in La Aquilla. I was the first one pulled out. I couldn't figure out why the medical staff, who were all Italian, got so excited. After all, I was a prisoner and I had malaria. The other eight men were German and probably wounded. They peeled back my tunic and shirt and looked puzzled. I looked down and saw all the blood on me. I pointed up at a German soldier. They dropped me in the hall and worked on the others.

I lay in the corridor for quite awhile, and I guess they looked after the wounded. I fell asleep again and woke up when an orderly and nurse began to strip and wash me. They gave me a pair of pyjamas and put me in a room with three Germans. One was an NCO. He told me not to escape and made a big deal about giving a young blond Jerry a Luger or a 38. At this time, I just wanted to sleep. I waved and acknowledged that I understood and shook and shivered some more and slept.

I can only remember eating cookies and a coffee substitute, which was tasty but not filling. I guess this was the start of my long hunger and the eventual loss of sixty-five pounds. I was around 170 pounds when I joined the army. When I finally escaped, I was 105.

The young German called over and smiled at me. He held up his automatic pistol and told me he was a paratrooper and had been injured in a jump nearby. He said that I was sure lucky to be going to Germany.

I think I was in the hospital for two weeks and was beginning to enjoy being in a bed with white sheets. One day a German soldier came to take me to my first prison camp. I was surprised to find that the camp was just around the corner. The hospital and camp were one complex. The barrack block was two stories high and made of brick. I was handed over to an English NCO. We went to the office, and I was registered and taken to the second floor and given a bunk and a blanket. I believe there were 5,000 POWs in the camp. A lot of them had fought in the desert and had been taken to Italy as POWs. When Italy capitulated, a lot of them escaped but were recaptured.

Most of the ones with food caches had been taken in the desert. I was the new kid on the block, but some of the fellows talked to me. I felt a little more at ease with all the friendly faces. I noticed, however, the ones with extra food, like the one in the bunk below me, were not friendly. I guess they thought they would be expected to share the food. I started to feel pangs of hunger. One of the things I craved was oatmeal, and I'll be damned if the guy below me didn't one day bring in a bowl and sat below me and ate it. I later found out the British Red Cross parcel had a small can of rolled oats in it. We were given a small loaf or bun a day, sometimes a piece of cheese or a bit of jam, but not everyday.

The soldiers from the British Indian forces served in the 8th Army in Africa and Italy. Those held captive with us would build a small fire on the ground and fry the chapattis the Red Cross sent. I wouldn't go near that spot. I was far too hungry to stand the aroma of fried bread. The Indians had to live on that food.

After roll call one day, I heard a commotion by the stairs. I watched a most disgusting thing. Three or four German officers were throwing cookies out to the POWs, and the POWs were fighting for them. For something like ten or twelve cookies among 100 or so men, they lowered themselves to animal level. I know they were no hungrier than me, but the German officers also lowered themselves, so one could expect anything from them.

There was nothing to do in this camp but plan to escape. This became my top priority. It was uppermost in my mind day and night. I was looking for a way to get out into the hills and to wait for the Allies. The desire to escape started the minute I was taken in Baranello and never ended. I figured the best way to escape was to do it when the chance came. Fifty years later a saying came up that hit the nail on the head: GO FOR IT.

One day in early November, we got word we were to go to Germany. I was with another Canadian chap from the Princess Dragoon Guards. We figured he was one of the men taken in the bunch I investigated when I got the V cigarettes. We heard someone playing the polonaise on a piano. The German sure could play, and we sat on the stairs and listened. Pretty soon two guards came along behind us. As we started to get up, they helped us down the steps with their boots. They had been looking for us. We had the distinction of being the last to leave the camp. As I left, I looked back, and it looked like the ground was waving. It was millions of fleas.

They crammed forty-five of us into a boxcar. There was not room for us all to sit at one time. Some stood while some sat and slept. They had wired off an area between the doors, and a guard had this to himself. Besides the cramped space, there was a half drum in each end for a toilet. Most of us had a touch of dysentery, and the drum splashed its contents over the side and made the trip very bad.

We travelled this way for six days and five nights. It was terribly cold going through the northern Italian Alps. We travelled through the Brenner Pass and into Germany with no coats or blankets. I thought we would freeze. At the time, I wished the Americans or RAF would bomb the tracks so we could make a break for Switzerland. I knew men would die or be injured, but not me. I'd get away! You never figure you will be one of them. I later learned one of the trains, of which there were five, was bombed.

When we finally stopped, we could barely walk to camp 7B. We arrived at Moosburg. There we had a shower, were deloused and waited for something to happen, and it did. The Germans rounded up all of us Canadians in the camp. The guards marched us to the train; I think there were ten or twenty of us plus two or three guards. We travelled from south Germany to just south of Berlin on a passenger train. After we got off the train, we marched to the camp.

5

Luckenwalde

For some reason, the Canadians were sorted out, and we were sent to an interrogation camp, Luckenwalde, just south of Berlin. This was not a pleasant place to be. Luckenwalde. Even the name seemed scary to me. We were assigned rooms, which turned out to be cells six feet wide by ten feet long and twelve feet high. Mine was room eight. It was built of concrete block and painted white. I'll never forget the feeling when that door slammed shut behind me.

There was a single wooden cot with a straw pad and a blanket, a small table and a stool. There was a high window with bars. I thought, at least it is clean. The guard showed me how to signal him if I had to use the toilet. There was a peephole with a levered cover so they could look in, and when I realized this, I moved my stool right up to the door so he couldn't see me. He would open the door, I would wave my hand and say hello. He would get mad and slam the door. No sense of humour. These doors were solid plank doors about two or more inches thick.

For a couple of days, a one-armed Russian brought me a bowl of soup. Then I was interrogated. A German officer questioned me about a new Canadian tank that I knew nothing about, then about troop movements. I asked him: "How much do German Generals tell their privates?"

He could see my point.

"You speak pretty good English," I said, as he had no accent.

"I should." He said. "I lived in Canada until the war." He had gone to Germany with his mother to visit, and then war was declared and he joined the army.

"You must know Germany is going to lose this war," I said,

"Win or lose, I'll go back to Toronto. I have a corner lot there, and I'm going to build a gas station on it," he replied. He also told me he could shoot me if I didn't answer his questions. He pulled out his Luger and put it on the desk in front of him.

"You wouldn't get any information out of me then, so it wouldn't do you any good." I said.

"It wouldn't do you much good either," he replied.

The next thing, he said, "I'll be right back." He walked around behind me to another room. He left his gun on the desk, so I figured it wasn't loaded. It was a trap to see if I would pick it up, and if I did, he had me where he wanted me. When he came back, he said, "I must be more careful" and put the gun in his holster. Then he tried to talk me into joining a special force of Allied prisoners assigned to go and fight the Russians. "We will give you two weeks leave with all the food and drinks and girls you want." It just happened that a man with a Canadian uniform and three stripes walked down the hall. He said, "There, he joined us." I said "No, thank you. I'm not a traitor."

"We'll all be fighting them soon," he said.

He called a guard and took me back to my cell. As I went out the door he said, "If you change your mind, just tell the guard."

I can't remember if it was the same day or the next when I heard screams out back. I put the stool on the table, climbed up and opened the window to the bars so I could see what was going on. There was an older man and a younger woman being beaten by some guards. The girl lay on the cement, and they were still working on the old man. When they both became unconscious, they turned a hose on them. This was in November. I'm sure they died out there.

Whether they spotted me or the guard looked in the peephole, I don't know, but the next thing that happened, I heard the door being unlocked.

Three big bruisers came through the door and circled me. One would hit me, then the other. I really don't know how long this went on, but I knew I was starting to lose consciousness and I was going down. Before I went out completely, they started to kick me and they didn't care where. I don't know how long I was unconscious. All I knew was it was dark, so dark I couldn't see my hands. There wasn't even light around the door. I don't know how they blacked out my cell. They may have moved me to another when I was unconscious. I groped around the cell trying to find my bed, but it was gone. No table or stool. I found a blanket with a big L-shaped tear in it. I couldn't see anything. The wall, nothing.

On top of this, I could feel my second bout of malaria coming on. I lay on the concrete floor for twenty days with malaria. You typically have four days with an extremely high fever. The little one-armed Russian delivered soup, but I could not eat when I had the fever. I don't even know if I had my soup all the time they blacked out my room. The food was equal to a Campbell's soup can a day and no bread, and I must have lost a lot of weight.

During later bouts and in better conditions with bed and blankets, my temperature would go to about 112° or 113° F (44 or 45° C). I had malaria eight times while I was a POW, but I think that was the worst bout. A cold concrete floor to lie on and a blanket with a hole in the middle in November. I remember lying, shaking and freezing but sweating.

I would curl up into a ball with my blanket with its big hole. I wondered when I was going to die, and how they would do it. I had lived through the beating. I was sure; especially after witnessing them kill two people. It was just a matter of time before they would do the same to me, I feared, if I didn't die from the effects of malaria. Why did I have to go through this first? Would they beat me out in the yard like the young woman and the old man?

When they finally opened the door, the guard came in yelling, "Raus, raus." He had to help me up, and I couldn't open my eyes. It was so bright. I thought, "At least I can't see them shoot me or whatever they are going to do." My belligerence started to cut in. It wasn't bravery; I was just damned mad. I decided to look them in the eye and spit on them, whatever they were going to do. Then I heard the familiar voice of Smoky Sealy. "George, I thought they killed you. I heard them, what they done."

Smoky took my arm and led me to the new area. He was crying. He thought they had blinded me because he heard them beating me. I said, "I think I'll be OK in a while." Smoky was a friend in need and a very feeling person. He led me by the arm. We followed a guard to a building that looked later, when I could see, like another stable. My eyes hurt, but my sight was coming back.

We followed a guard to a large room. Smoky found a couple of bunks. He got me a bottom bunk. We all sat around and talked. They said the guys at the other end were all officers, including a brigadier who had been in charge of the Dodecanese group of islands. I was told he gave them up without a fight. There were half a dozen other officers including a colonel and a doctor.

Later on the brigadier called a parade. This guy still had his batman and camp cot. They had had their tea, and perhaps he thought he should do something to show his authority. I guess it gave him a feeling of power or importance. He stopped in front of me, tore a strip off of me for not shaving and being very unsoldierly. I told him I didn't have a razor, that I was captured while I was fighting the enemy and scouting in the front. "I didn't carry my razor."

"Borrow one." He said.

"Under K.R. Can, I can't do that." I said

"Under what?" he asked.

"Kings Regulations, Canada." I replied.

Then he gave me a dressing-down for quoting King's rules and for insubordination. He would report me when we got to a registered POW camp. I said I would do the same. Brockford, another Canadian from the Ontario tank battalion, tried to get the doctor to look at me. He refused. Later, we talked about this high-ranking bunch, and I said,

"He is worried that I haven't shaved; I haven't even washed my hands or face for a month." We got a chuckle out of that.

6

POW Camp

I THINK IT WAS the next day, maybe two. We left to go to Stalag 4B, Mülhberg, on the Elbe in the State of Brandenburg. I don't think anyone was sorry to leave that pompous little brigadier behind. Besides, we all had an uneasy feeling about Luckenwalde. I have often thought that the month in Luckenwalde had to be the worst period in my life.

We arrived at Mülhberg a little before Christmas. The camp was in the German mountains, and there was snow on the ground. It was cold and we had no coats. When going to a different camp, you have a shower in a room five or six metres square with shower heads all over the ceiling. It sure felt good. Our clothes went through a delousing. The barber ran the clippers over our heads and took off our hair. When the Germans shaved off your hair, they didn't take your beard. Germans seemed only to do what they were told. I guess they weren't told about beards. We had mug shots taken, front and side. "If I shave off my beard and my hair grows back, the picture is no good," I thought. But that was how the Germans were.

We were registered and became official POWs. I was now 263730. We even got dog tags to wear around our necks. We got issue of razor, blades and a brush and a comb. Well, we could comb our beards, as we had no hair.

A little English corporal with a clipboard said as he passed:

"Register as corporal or higher. They don't have to work." So we did. I came out a corporal. The rest of them promoted themselves up to regimental sergeant majors, although I don't think some would make lance corporal in the real world.

We were taken to a barracks, and the Canadians were split up. Some went to the Indian hut next to the one I was in. We were all so tired; we slept as soon as we got our usual three-foot-high bunk.

I remember walking into the barracks in this camp. They had Christmas decorations corner-to-corner, red and green. They were made from salmon can labels from the Canadian Red Cross parcels. I learned very early on that the Canadian parcels were the best. They had cans of salmon, corn beef, Spam, beans, butter and a package of pilot biscuits. The trouble was we should have gotten them each week, but it was far from it.

I was put in with the British. The group I

mucked in with had all been taken in North Africa. They were nice guys, one Scot and two English, one from the Newcastle area. All their stories were interesting. The big Scot was a professional soldier in the Scots Guards. Before being posted to the desert, he got a forty-eight-hour pass and went home to the Highlands to say goodbye to his wife. He told her he was off to fight the war. She said, "Why don't you leave that up to the army." She was apparently oblivious to the fact that the guards were part of the army.

The Scot had been run over by one of his own trucks and was sent down the line to the hospital. He escaped from the hospital when he felt better and returned to his outfit just in time for a big push by the Germans. He was taken prisoner then.

I'll never understand the British. Even in a prison camp deep inside enemy territory, they fought each other. The gangs would beat up one of the other gangs. There was the Liverpool gang, the Glasgow gang, the Irish gangs. Over time, there were several beatings. So we Canadians got together and sent a three-man delegation to each of the leaders. We told them that if a Canadian was touched, the leaders would be the ones who would pay the price, the price being found in the cess-pool of the toilet, or over the fence. Either place he would die. After that, we didn't have a problem with them.

The violence was not confined to the British, however. Two of the Indians had an argument, and unfortunately one of them walked past the other in the third-tier bunk and lost an ear. They certainly kept the razors sharp.

We had to thank the Indian soldiers for our Red Cross parcels, however. In this camp the British officers were senior in the chain of command. They wouldn't issue the new Canadians a parcel. The reason, in British military thinking, was that we weren't on strength when the parcels were delivered. The Indian hut refused their Red Cross parcel and went on a hunger strike until we got ours. So they relented and gave us our parcel. My bunch had shared with me, but it was just the thought. I was getting fed up with the British military after the brigadier in the last camp, and now this bunch. What really made us mad was that they were Canadian Red Cross parcels.

But all said, I fell in with a good group. They welcomed me. The whole room welcomed me. Life in this camp with the friends I made was good compared to what I went through in Luckenwalde. I had a feeling of relative safety. I was still surprised that I was alive, so I took each day as it came and planned a new escape.

We had Christmas 1943 in Mülhburg. I made a plum duff with pilot biscuits and some dried fruit with thick Klim (milk) poured over it. I did this by grating the pilot biscuits into flour and mixing in milk. Then we placed it in the ash pit of the heater. The six of us who shared my concoction spent the rest of the day running to the toilet.

I also spent my twenty-first birthday in this camp. Although I didn't realize it was my birthday until about eight or nine o'clock in the evening.

One day I watched a half-dozen Russians searching the garbage cans for food. A German officer walked by. The Russians didn't come to attention and salute, so he punched each one in the face. When they stood up, he hit them again. This kept on until they couldn't get up.

I'm not sure how long we stayed at the camp, but one day they rounded up all of the Canadians and sent us to a new camp, Stalag 2B west of Hammerstein in western Prussia. We didn't stay long. I think they changed their minds and shipped us to Stalag 357, a camp in the Polish Corridor called Thorn. While we were at 2B, a funny thing happened. A guard took a bunch of us out to dig fence posts. We dug some, and they moved us to the next road. One of the barrack room lawyers said:

"They can't make us build outside fences."

We thought, "That's right. They can't."

We can build inside fences to divide the compound, but not outside fences. The ground was hard. There were hard bits of snow and ice still on the ground. We told the German officer we didn't have to build outside fences.

"Dig," he said.

"No," we said

"Dig," he said.

"No," we said.

We were getting quite a kick out of it until he took off his hat and threw it in the mud and jumped on it. At the same time, he took out his gun. Thinking he was mad enough to kill, we decided we better dig. We sent a man to see the Commandant, however. While our man was in the Commandant's office, one man would dig a hole, then the next man would fill it in, the next would dig it out again. In the end, the Commandant agreed with us and took us off all fence-post digging.

On the way to one of the camps, I don't remember which one; we saw a lot of men in uniforms we didn't recognize. The guard said they were Spanish going to Russia. On two other moves, we encountered groups of Hitler youth. They would jeer and taunt and spit at us. The guard couldn't do anything because the leader would report him. When we were out of sight, he would make signs that he didn't like them.

We moved to Thorn soon after the post-digging incident. Once again, it was all the Canadians.

7

The Polish Corridor

We travelled to Stalag 357 in the Polish Corridor, in the usual way: boxcar. When we reached it, we were really surprised. Here was a fairly new camp that could hold 10,000 men and eventually did. It was empty, just twenty Canadians. For the first time, the Germans came into the hut and counted us instead of making us stand outside at 6 a.m. freezing. This didn't last long, of course. As more prisoners came in, they paraded us.

We had an older guard, the equivalent of a company sergeant major who sort of befriended us Canadians. We had been at the camp a month or so, and one day he came in and broke down. He had been away for a week. He told us his wife had been killed at a train station. She fell in front of a train, but he swore that the Gestapo pushed her. She had told him she had been watched and followed. He didn't know what she was suspected of. Neither did she. But it cost her her life. After that he would get us just about anything he could, like a radio. I think he didn't want to live under the Gestapo. To live in fear all the time would be hell. It is strange, but people will know about things like the Gestapo, however, until it affects someone close, they look the other way and hope it won't affect them.

I think Stalag 357 in Poland was the best-organized camp that I was in. Life wasn't too unpleasant. Our wooden huts were divided into smaller rooms with twelve men to a room. We walked the outer track. Everyone walked anti-clockwise except for two of us. When they said we were going the wrong way, we said we meet more people this way.

I did meet a lot of people, including a spirited Newfoundlander who was billeted in our barrack. He would jump out of bed in the morning and look out the window and say, "Lord Jasis Garge! Ders tousands and tousands of herring in the bay. There must be fi hunert." He was a great guy, but there was no water for 500 miles.

Several things happened here, from stage shows to escape committees. We saw the V1s or V2s being tested. We couldn't figure out what they were. Our friendly guard said it was Hitler's little secret weapon.

Once we ate a guard dog, a Doberman. He

attacked the wrong man, a Canadian trapper. He snapped its neck. It was tough meat, but the broth was strengthening. Boy was Jerry mad.

It was in Stalag 357 that I learned to mould lead. A POW said sand would be good for making a mould, so I scrounged some boards to make one and asked all the men to save the lead paper wrapping from the tobacco packages. I borrowed a hat badge from a Seaforth and made a mould of it. When I had enough, I melted the wrapping down in a tin cup on a small forge. By this time I had a few interested fellows watching. To our amazement, it came out perfect on the second try.

I had experience as a tin basher (tin smith) from my shipyard training. I borrowed some scissors and made cups from Canadian butter tins. I melted the lead from cigarette packages to make the rivets tight and made plates by joining two pieces of tin.

I also made blowers, small forges we used to cook on. They were like the small forges used in blacksmith shops and had a small fan run by a string belt system. With very little fuel, we could boil water or reheat the soup, as it always reached us lukewarm. I don't know how many I made, but I improved on each one as I went on. All of the material in the tins of Klim, butter, salmon and Spam from the Canadian Red Cross parcels was first-class. I became quite good at building blowers, and I had one geared down to the point that I could blow the wood right out of the firebox.

Once I made a very large blower, and just as I assembled it, the Camp Commandant made an inspection. I suppose he thought it was some kind of a tunnel ventilation system. He said: "Was ist dos infernal machine?" I showed him what is was for, but he did not believe me and confiscated it. From then on, all blowers were infernal machines. One of the fellows called my operation, "Reid's Infernal Machine Company."

Things got organized. A little theatre group put on a play. They used Red Cross tea crates for props. It gave a lot of fellows something to do. Boxes had to be pried apart, formed into props and painted. The play was planned to go on long enough so that everyone had a chance to see it. There was a feeling of excitement in the air. Fellows kidded about getting a haircut and polishing their shoes to go to the theatre. The camp Commandant was invited and was amazed at the costumes, all made by the tailors in the costume department from uniforms, blankets and what the guards could bring in. He didn't know, of course, that the same people also made clothes for escapes. Well, the show was a hit. What else could it be? It was good, so good it had to be closed down. A twenty-four-hour guard even had to be put on the young fellow who played the part of the female.

Also at the camp, an American tried to escape against the wishes of the escape committee. The Germans held him at gunpoint for several hours between the two outside fences. Then about dawn, they shot him where he stood.

While at Stalag 357, I was in the camp hospital several times with malaria. My malaria seemed to hit harder than ever. I was in what we called a hospital as much as I was out. It took twenty days to go through a bout of it and a day or two of rest. I was in three weeks, and out three weeks. In the next room was one of Tito's men from Yugoslavia. He was out of his head and he would yell and scream and fight the doctors or whoever he was near. Two RAF gunners, both ex-wrestlers, took turns holding him down when he went off the deep end.

One morning I came out of a deep sleep and was surprised to see one of the RAF fellows sitting on a chair next to my cot. As usual, I was wringing wet.

"Hi Jock, What's up?"

"You're all right then, Canada?"

"I think so. Why?"

"You were off your head for a bit, so I had to make sure you didn't hurt yourself. I thought we had another one like Tito in there."

Then I remembered the snakes coiled around the rafters.

"So, that was what it was, was it?" Jock said

I guess it was at the end of a four-day bout that I became delirious. I had been delirious before, but not that bad.

During the last attack they gave me all the quinine they had. The doctor said it was half a treatment, but it seemed to do the trick for quite a while. For some reason, I lost partial use of my feet while I had one of my bouts. I could not raise my foot when I walked and would drag my toes unless I raised my knees quite high. It did not last long, but it scared me just the same.

Finally, they moved the whole camp further west to Örbke, Germany, as the Russians were getting too close. The camp number, Stalag 357, was the same. The barracks were big and barn-like, and it was cold.

Stalag 2D, Stargard

A SHORT TIME BEFORE we Canadians were transferred to Stalag 2D, they tried to move the whole camp again. The word was we were going to Stalag 8B, but on the way something went wrong. I believe we were in the Russians' path again. We sat in the marshalling yards in Hanover. This was a Sunday morning, and everyone knew that at 1 P.M. the Americans bombed the Hanover marshalling yards. So Hanes and I ate our two-day ration of black bread. We said we were going to die on a full stomach. We no sooner finished the bread than the train started. We heard the bombs dropping behind us. We landed back in 357 the next day. I got a bad time from Hanes because we didn't have anything to eat.

One day they called a parade. All the Canadians were called out, and we were presented with our Canadian service medals and clasp. The damn fools sent our name, number and rank, so all the phoney NCOs were transferred to a camp about five miles away. We walked to it.

We talked a guard into bringing in a violin because we had a chap who had played with the Vancouver symphony. Even with all those men, you could hear a pin drop when he played.

In this camp, I traded some Ex-lax for a loaf of bread from a guard named Hans. The next night, he wasn't on guard, so I asked the replacement: "Where is Hans?"

He said, "Hans ist krank (sick). Ja, ist scheissen, scheissen."

The training camp across the road gave us some fun. The Jerries marched up and down doing the goose step. We would call out, "Quack, Quack." This went on for a while. One day the German CO told us we had to stop saying "Quack, Quack."

This camp was terribly overcrowded. The barrack was posted to hold seventy men and there were close to 400. All twenty-five of the Canadians lived in one hut. The bunks were three tiers head to toe, side by side, with an aisle every second row. The beds were made with sackcloth covering wood and straw. Most of the bottom bunks had two men. It was cozy.

I hadn't realized we were near the sea. If I could have got away, I might have made it. Each day I planned a break. Each time we moved, I watched for a chance to break out. I was convinced that this was the way to do it. See a chance and take it.

One of the Canadians, Jack (I don't know his last name), became friendly with some Americans and decided to move to their building. A few days later, the SS raided the camp. They did this quite often. The regular guards would rush into the huts and chase everyone out. On this particular raid, they chased everyone out onto the parade ground then they searched the building. We were then told to go back and stand by our beds. As we came back in, they searched us. Then they searched two beds. In the second one, they found a 38 revolver. It was Jack's bed.

They didn't search any more beds after that. One would think if they found one gun, they would look for more. That would be the natural thing to do. I know it wasn't his, but they took him to a cell in the army camp across the road. He was found guilty and sentenced to be shot. Under the Geneva Convention, they had to wait six months, I think. I don't know if he made it, but by this time the war had ended.

I had a run-in with another Englishman, Regimental Sergeant Major Lord. We were being counted, 10,000 of us. I was talking to the fellow behind me. The next thing I knew, this RSM is asking if I want a special invitation to come to attention.

So I said, "If you're giving them, yes. Because I don't come to attention for German corporals. I'm still fighting them."

"See me in my office after parade," he said to me.

I'll never forget that meeting. There was this damned big Airborne RSM uniform like it just came out of the cleaners. Boots polished. He was about six-foot-four, with red hair that I'm sure got redder the madder he got. I do know his neck got redder. It looked like a thermometer. He started to roll up his sleeves, and I thought he was going to take a round out of me, so I backed up to the heater. If he swung, he'd have to get me the first time because I'd crown him with the poker. Well, I was thinking so much about getting my clock cleaned and the poker, I was surprised when he turned and washed his face.

Long after the war, I read a book called *A Bridge Too Far* and other written pieces about Lord. The British rewarded him with an MBE for bringing high standards to the camp. I didn't see it that way, and I discovered that others felt the same way as I did. Well, I could see he just didn't like Canadians, or Aussies or Kiwis for that matter, and I had my doubts about the Yanks.

The Salt Mines

A FEW DAYS AFTER our set-to, all the Canadians were sent to a work camp. This camp was a *bestrafung* or punishment camp. I figure it was because of my encounter with RSM Lord. The way I reckoned, he ran the camp and the Germans wanted so many men to work and he chose us. We were loaded onto the back of a truck and were transported throughout the night. At daybreak we arrived at a small site of about six or seven huts including the cookhouse and guards barracks. There were two huts for what we called "Ruskies." They were all women, and surprisingly, most had auburn hair. We found out they worked in an ammunition factory, and the cordite discoloured their hair.

Later in the morning, we went to work; we walked about two miles. On the right was the ammunition factory, on the left were Quonset huts covered with sod and trees. We found out it was the biggest German ammunition dump at that time. Every few nights, we would hear the Mosquito bombers flying low over the camp. We hoped they wouldn't find the dump.

On the way to work, we speculated about what kind of work we would be doing. There were many trees in the area, so there was speculation that it might have been a lumber camp. I kept asking the old guard what kind of *arbeit* (work) we would be doing. He kept saying what sounded like "Salts grooby." Each time I asked, he just said "Salts grooby." I guess I was pretty dumb. We rounded a stone wall, and I saw the big wheels over the shaft of a mine. I saw a high stone wall up ahead on the right. When we entered the big iron gate, it all came to me. A mine. A salt mine. My mind raced. "My God," I said. "It's a salt mine." The guys around laughed and kidded me.

"This isn't Russia. We aren't in Siberia"

But I knew what it was. I recalled my mother telling me of her cousin coming back from the World War I broken and old before his time from crawling in small tunnels of a salt mine in Russia. He was so bent that she didn't recognize him.

We were herded into a two-story lift or elevator. One double cage went down then the other passed half-way. We passed the empty cage. It seemed an eternity. I had never been so deep in the Earth, and I don't think any of the others had. I began to think the Lord had answered the prayers I had said when I was digging slit trenches to get away from Jerry's 88 mm and machine guns.

We had to wait at the bottom of the shaft for the rest. I tasted the rocks: salt crystals. The fears I had up top left. These shafts were seven- to eight-feet high. Finally we hit the bottom and we got out of the cage at the 2,800-foot level. When the rest of the fellows arrived, a miserable little man handed out the tools: pick, sixteen-pound hammers and shovels. He gave a speech saying, "This is Deutsch-land, and in Deutschland there is no strikes."

I was handed a shovel, and I said, "Was ist das?"

"Schaufel," he said.

"Schaufel? Nicht schaufel."

He took it out of my hand and said something, I'm sure, about the ignorance and stupidity of Canadians. He tried to show me how it worked.

"Ah, in Canada is nicht schaufel. All ist machine." I said.

This fellow looked at me and repeated, "All ist machine?" He looked as if he couldn't wait to get to Canada.

"Nicht schaufel. All is machine," I said.

A few weeks later, he beat the hell out of me with a pick handle. He said I spit at him. Spit! I didn't have enough fluid in me to spit. I thought he was going to kill me. So did the rest of the boys. They stopped him, I don't know how as I was on the ground. I think he must have told someone with a little more grey matter about his post-war immigration plan, and they told him the facts of life, and so my beating. So much for German humour. I was helped up and went back to work.

But I am getting ahead of my story. We left the cage and walked down the shaft on the right. A tunnel had been dug, and railway tracks and a steel door had been embedded in the salt. About thirty men were behind this. They were political prisoners as well as criminals and murderers. Some had twenty-year sentences. This was the night shift. They were allowed to go up to the surface every second Sunday for two hours, but most of them didn't bother. By the time their eyes became accustomed to the light, they had to go back down. We had a pretty good idea how they felt because all that winter it was dark when we went back to the camp. At 6 P.M. they blasted, and all day we moved the lumps of salt. If it was too big, we broke it up with hammers. I was down to just over 100 pounds at this time. At just over 100 pounds, a sixteen-pound hammer is a pretty cumbersome tool. Besides this, our morale was low. We didn't know how the war was going.

We had every second Sunday off. We worked from 6 A.M. to 6 P.M. We had to leave the camp by 5 and returned around 7. Then we would try to wash the salt off ourselves. Sometimes we had soap, but not always. When we had a Sunday off, a lot of fellows just spent it in the bunk resting.

Some of the guards could be very kind, or even compassionate. Like the guard who had been a POW in World War I. He would bring an extra sandwich each day when I was in the salt mine and give half of one to a different man. He told us this was because a Canadian soldier threw him a can of bully beef when he was a POW.

A bit more about the mine. We were not mining the salt for any use. We were building a factory. The main shaft was quite large, about ten-by-ten feet in this area. Shafts went off alternatively, one on the right, one on the left, one on the right, etc. I think there were five or six rooms. These shafts led into large rooms. One room I paced out was 300 feet long by 100 feet wide. I estimated the height to be twenty to twenty-five feet high. The lighting at this time was just two wires around the wall with bulbs every fifty or so feet. With the white and light grey salt, it didn't take a lot of bulbs to illuminate it enough to do the kind of work we were doing.

The rumour was it was going to be a Focke-Wolfe aircraft factory, but in retrospect, I would think the V2s would be more likely to be built in it. If they ever got into production, it could never be bombed. Later on, after the war, I heard that the Germans had come up with the first jet fighter. So who knows, this could have been meant to build the jets. By the time we left, the state prisoners and we had concrete floors down, tracks in, loading platforms. But it would take a lot of work yet, like heavy wiring and all the things required for manufacturing.

Before the Canadians got on the job, they used Russian women down there. The guard would always lament that five Russian women could do more than twenty Canadians. The reason was probably because we worked at slowing things down. We would kick an electric extension onto the track and run over it with the mine cars. This would cause a blackout, and we would work like heck to hide some shovels and picks in the mine cars under some salt. When the lights came on we would be sitting down, quite innocent. We would dump the cars down the old shaft, and when we got back to the loading area, we would look for our tools, and then call the little Jerry.

"Nicht schaufel, etc." Then he would look. This all took time. Sometimes we would put an extra large chunk into the car. It would take four or five of us and would jam the hole we dumped the load into. Then we would have to clear it with pry bars and hammers. The mine cars were larger than any I've seen in Canada. They were six-by-six feet at the top and tapered to a sort of V with a round bottom. You could get quite a load. You could also tip it to get a very large chunk into it. We had a quota of thirteen cars per man, which meant 260 cars. It didn't matter if five guys were working on the concrete mixer. There were still twenty of us. We quite often passed out, especially on the mixer. It was electric, and if things got too bad, they would give the sign and someone would short out the power.

While loading the large chunks into the mine cars, I hurt my back. Unable to rest, my back always irritated me with these heavy loads. We worked twelve hours a day, thirteen days out of fourteen. We had a bowl of soup a day and a slice of bread. At first it was about one-and-one-quarter inches thick. By the end, it was between one-half to three-quarters of an inch thick. We did various jobs in the mine from drilling holes to blast at the end of the shift, to breaking the big lumps into little lumps with a sixteen-pound hammer, loading mine cars. We had a quota of thirteen cars per man per day. We also mixed concrete for the floors. While doing the concrete work, we often collapsed or fainted. That was the only time we got water. It was steady work, and we had to keep up with the machine. The only break was when someone shorted the lights.

Once, while we waited for the rest of the crew on the surface, we walked around the compound and found a pigsty with a few pigs and a pile of partly rotten turnips. We stole some turnips and marked the pigs for later on, when the war ended. We would periodically check on them. This was where we met some of the Ruski women who worked below. We figured it would be a race to get to the pigs, but maybe we could have had a banquet for us all.

The little guy in charge of us was a coal miner, and he had pockmarks of coal in his face. Like a lot of small men, he didn't like anyone taller than him. The fact that he was a Kraut without a sense of humour, and just naturally mean, and we weren't doing our best for the Fuehrer didn't help his disposition. This little man had singled me out as a troublemaker, and he beat me a few times. I don't know if someone pointed me out or the little man just suspected me. When the lights came back on after a blackout, he would come straight to me and beat the daylights out of me with a pick handle. He wouldn't stop until I was on the floor of the shaft. I remember the different sounds the club made depending on what part of me he hit. I don't know if he or the rest of the men noticed, and it could have been my imagination, but as I was going down, I could not help but think he could play a tune on my bones.

One day he singled me out again. He must have thought I was the reason for all the foul-ups. He let me have it again with the pick handle. I think he liked the sound of the damned thing hitting my bones.

Later on, after I had had my fun with the guard

and after the guard had his fun with me, and after I came to, I was sentenced to twelve hours in the saltpetre room. This happened early in the shift, around 8. We called the dusty room the "saltpetre room," but it was not really saltpetre. It was a vein of soft or dusty salt. No one worked in the saltpetre room more than two hours because of the salt dust. You could not see the other side of the room. After two hours your eyes stung. You found blood in the mucous from your nose. He kept me in the room from 8 A.M. until 6 P.M. All I could see was red. My eyes were so sore I couldn't close them. When I did, I couldn't bear to open them. My nose was bleeding, even one of my ears bled. My throat felt like someone ran a wire brush down it, and I coughed up blood. The guys had to help me back to the camp that night.

I believe I might have done him some harm if things hadn't happened as they did in the end. In retrospect, if it wasn't for that little Kraut, things could have been pretty good down there. After all, it was warm, dry, and I didn't have another bout of malaria while I was there. I had a running wound on my left calf from the shrapnel on my scouting trips. Gas gangrene had set in, and it ran pus and smelled like heck. Before I went to the mine, I could stick my thumb in the hole past the first joint. After two or three weeks in the salt mines, it had healed.

10

Escape

O<small>N SATURDAY APRIL</small> 7, 1945, we finished our shift and the inevitable roll call and count. They informed us that we would be evacuating the camp. We got the news with our soup and bread that, on Monday, we would be evacuating the camp and that we would be doing this on foot. As it was our Sunday off, we should rest up.

We had heard stories of these forced marches. The rumours were that if you fell out and couldn't go on, Jerry just shot you. I thought all this over and decided to try to escape. I didn't think I would last. I was down to 105-pounds. If I came down with malaria, I was finished. I didn't think I would live through the march. We didn't know how long we would have had to keep moving, and it was either be shot on the march or be shot trying to escape.

When I decided to try to escape, I did what most escapees did. I went to the rest of the men. I started to put in action a plan that I had thought of earlier. But I would need a bit of cooperation from the rest of the fellows. The field across the street could be used for soccer or softball if we wished on our day off. Usually, no one had the strength to go. I asked in each of the rooms for help. At first I was disappointed, but I guess the fellows thought about it and six men came to me one at a time and said:

"Speed, (my nickname) I can get three or two or four to go out if you take me with you." I had to stop at six. I was the seventh. The group was getting too big. The bigger the break, the easier it would be to detect it. After I counted all the guys they could take, it came to a dozen more than we had on strength. I guess some doubled up. Anyway, I think the whole camp turned out.

All night I thought and planned. That night, we had a meeting. I told the other six to save bread rations and whatever food they could take in their pockets. No bags. (As it was, we didn't need bags because we didn't have that much food.) The plan was simple. While the barracks were surrounded with the usual rows of barbed wire, the field was not. We would kick the ball into the bush. Four or five would run in to get it. One of us would stay in the bush, and the rest would come out with the ball until all the escapees were in the bush. The fellows seemed to think it might work.

Sunday morning came. We had meetings, we

got ready to either go or back off. I for one knew there was no turning back. We rested until the afternoon and said our goodbyes to our buddies. They wished us well. Then the time came. We straggled over to the field so the guards would have trouble getting a proper count. The guards were posted around the field. We started to play. The ball would be kicked at the goal and then would go into the bush. Our side would claim a goal. The other side would say "No goal." They would bring the guard into it to see if he saw it. In the ensuing argument, we got a couple more into the bush, and so on until we all arrived.

I was the last to go. The rendezvous was a power-line pole, and they hid all around. When I got there, we took off. My plan was to head west and hopefully find the Allies, or at least to hide out in the bush. As soon as I got there, we took off and headed west, following the sun.

Our first obstacle was a work group marching up the road we had to cross. We watched a few minutes, and I spotted a trail across the road, so I said, "Do as I do and follow me." With a lot of luck, we crossed the road and walked through the work gang. The trail was well used. We acted as if we were going home.

When we got out of sight, we ran as far as we could to make up for lost time. We jumped into the brush when a Jerry came down on a bike. We lay there until he passed. We hit the road again, but walking now, too tired to run. Then we heard the dogs. We knew who they were looking for. I can tell you there is nothing on earth that will give you energy like dogs barking and howling and knowing that they are after you. Jerry used Alsatians and Dobermans. It didn't really matter to me which breed was howling and barking. We all looked at each other, and one of the guys said, "Let's go." We started to jog so we could stay together.

I think someone was watching over us that Sunday afternoon because we came to a ditch running right and left of the path. It was a deep drainage ditch around a farm. It had six or eight inches of water in it. As the leader of the group, I had to make a decision. I said, "If we stick together, we may all be caught. If we split up, some of us may make it." One of the fellows spoke passable German, so I said, "You go with those three. We'll go this way." We ran along the ditch to lose the scent. By the time we left the ditch it started to get dark, and we didn't have to worry. The fields had a couple of inches of water on them, so we felt we had lost the dogs.

We left the ditch and went across the field. The three of us walked a good part of the night. It is still cold in central Europe in April. Our feet were soaked, our pants were soaked. It wasn't too bad while we walked, but we had to stop sometime. We found a haystack and tried to burrow into it. We couldn't get far. So we pulled as much as we could get off, too tired to get under some. We weren't too successful. We damned near froze. In the morning, I couldn't get any feeling in my feet. We left at daylight, and it was noon by the time I could feel my feet. Of course, they were wet, and I know there was ice on my pants. I was damn sure there was ice on my socks, but I figured if I took my boots off, I wouldn't get them back on. I sure needed them if I was going to go much further.

We forced ourselves to walk. One day we walked on a trail with young fir trees. I think it must have been a reforestation area as the trees were planted in straight lines. Once we walked at night in a farming area. These were groups of buildings. It looked as if several farms were joined to form a commune or small village. Once, we came across a parachute harness hanging in a tree. Then the third day, it was dull. The sun was all we had to go by, so we walked the way we thought was west. We had walked two or three hours when one fellow, Joe Cronan, said, "Speed, have you ever seen the sun come up from the west?"

I said, "No, not to my knowledge,"

Joe said, "Well, it did today or we're going the wrong way." He had just caught a glimpse of the sun through the heavy cloud cover. We had guessed that morning which way to go. We had guessed wrong, but perhaps it was meant to be. We turned back and retraced our steps for a while. We were travelling along a nice country road with large trees on either side. Suddenly, we came up to a truck parked at the side of the road. We had captured one like it, the one I got the large pair of binoculars out of. We could hear the Germans inside. We move by silently, like we were on patrol, in case a guard was on duty. I guess they felt secure, as they didn't post a guard.

Next day we walked down a back road in a new forest, and for some reason we took a road going off to the right. We followed it about half a mile when three young Germans, about fourteen to sixteen years old stepped out onto the road. They had army uniforms on, but they were just kids. "Don't panic," I said, "Don't run. They couldn't miss at this distance. We'll try to bluff it out." I was hoping that one of them didn't want to end the war without killing something. Like us. They asked us a bunch of questions, but I played dumb and pointed back saying "Arbeit, Arbeit, work, work." I don't think they bought it because they grinned and shook their heads.

Just then, a car came up the road. The young soldiers flagged him down, and the driver got out of the car. He listened to the soldiers. "Are you English?" he asked

"Canadian," I said.

He looked surprised and asked what we were doing there. We said we were just out for a walk. He translated that, but the boys wouldn't buy it. He introduced himself and said he was a doctor and that the soldiers didn't seem to believe me. He seemed like a decent sort, so I grinned and hunched my shoulders. He smiled and said, "I have to put my car away, and then I will come back."

The soldiers asked him if he would take us up to the village and lock us in the village jail. He asked if we would go with him. We said sure. I think it showed the lack of training. These kids were going to have to go into battle against trained men. I hope they had enough sense to hide in the bush when the Allies came through.

I asked the doctor to translate a message to the boys. I said the war is almost over and Germany has lost. If they try to fight, they will be killed. If any Allied army comes, hide in the trees. There had been too many lives lost and too much blood shed.

The doctor took his car home. We had stumbled into an area where city types had built cabins or cottages in the new and not so new forest. They all seemed to be occupied. Later, the doctor told us he and his wife and little boy were bombed out of their house in Berlin. This was a summer retreat for city dwellers. When he came back, we returned to the village with him.

"Are you sure you were not escaping?" he asked.

"We would like to, but I think the front is too far away," I replied.

"Not really," he said.

Just at that moment, we heard heavy machine guns. The doctor stopped. "That's the Americans now."

"How long has it been since you had a good meal?" he asked.

"A year and a half," I replied.

"Good God," he said after we told him how we were fed and that we had to work for twelve hours a day. I told him what we ate and about the salt mine. I think he was truly amazed. I added that we felt we had been well treated in relation to the treatment of the Russians and Poles.

"I had no idea they treated you fellows so badly. Come and I will take you to my home." He said. "I will see what I can find to feed you."

He must have been a trusting person, because he took us to his home and introduced us to his wife and left. We could have murdered her and his little boy for all he knew. He returned in about fifteen minutes with some food. He said he had to go to five houses to get enough to feed three of us. His wife cooked us a meal. She would see an army truck and say, "Is this the Americans, George?"

I'd look and say "No, that's your side."

During this time, a Jerry came to the door. He asked if they saw any escaped POWs. Fortunately, the doctor's wife had seen him as he approached, and we hid. I was behind a door with a two-foot piece of firewood. It was going to be him or me at this point, but he didn't come in.

About twenty minutes later, a self-propelled half-track 88 mm came down the road, and I watched them set it up just on the far side of a stone bridge. It was about 700 or 800 yards away, and I figured, "It wouldn't be long now." Fortunately, there was a curve in the road that allowed us to see both ways. From the other direction we could see the Americans coming. Their first four or five vehicles were Jeeps, no match for an 88 mm.

"George, George. This is them," she called. It was and I ran.

I told Joe and the other chap that I should run over to warn the Yanks, to get these folks into the forest and over the bank into cover. At the house, we could see up the road. It came down and turned at a 50° or 60° bend. When I ran across the field, Jerry spotted me and opened up with their machine guns. The 88 mm guns always had machine guns to protect them from the infantry. I dove for the ground. I got up and ran. I did this several times. Finally, I dove into the ditch. There was an awful lot of lead flying. My luck still held, and I made it to a ditch by the road. When I looked up, I was looking up the barrel of an American machine gun. I said: "For God's sake, don't shoot." I suppose I looked pretty scared. The young lieutenant told the gunner, a black man, to put it up. He said, "Who are you and what is all the shooting?"

I told him I was a Canadian Seaforth Highlander. He said, "Your front is over yonder by the coast." I said, "Mine was in Italy. I took a short-cut. But the point is, there is an 88 set up down the road." The lieutenant called up something heavier. In the meantime, I explained I was an escaped POW. Soon five tanks lumbered up. I showed the leader where the 88 was on the map. They all backed up the road, turned their guns to right angles and thundered back past us. They must have been doing fifty when they rounded the curve. They started firing as soon as they cleared the trees. I don't know which tank got the gun, but the Jerry ambush went up in a cloud of black smoke and an explosion.

The American boys couldn't do enough for me. They didn't lose a man. There were cheers, and they were shaking my hand and slapping me on the back. I remember the few men in the first Jeeps cheering and patting me on the shoulder and thanking me for stopping them from sure death. I felt I got my last licks in at Jerry, and I think I saved a lot of American lives, or at least a lot of suffering on their part. Later, the lieutenant asked if he could do anything for me. I had all the K rations I could eat. I said I'd sure appreciate some food to take to the doctor and his wife and baby.

"Would they eat K rations, do you think?" he asked.

I wish I knew the doctor's name, the name of the village or even the area. And I wish I knew the American outfit we ran into. I believe it was the 3rd Armoured. Other than Joe, I don't know the names of the fellows who escaped with me. I never even got a letter of thanks for saving so many lives and putting my own life at risk. Perhaps the officer in charge didn't report the incident.

We moved down to the hotel where the 88 mm was and took it over. A woman, I think she was the cook, ran into the hotel and told us not to drink the beer, that it had been poisoned by the Bürger-meister who was also the manager or owner of the hotel. He was found, and we considered making him drink it. He refused. Poisoning is outlawed by the Geneva Convention Rules of War. He was a real Nazi type. He even combed his hair like the Fuhrer. He was held in custody, and the next day he was shot trying to escape.

That night we slept in a hotel room with a bed and blankets. Man was that living it up. We even had K rations in the room in case we got hungry. The next day we returned to HQ where American and British intelligence people questioned us. We told them about the ammunition dump and the ammunition factory near the camp we just left. This dump was supposed to be the largest in

Germany's arsenal. It went on for miles. They said they had been looking for it, so I told them that our camp was in the corner of it and that whenever we heard the Mosquito bombers fly over at night, we prayed they didn't find it. I asked them to make sure the camp was empty before they started to bomb it.

The questioning was over, so the Americans wanted to ship us back. The lieutenant told us they ran into the rest of our group up the road but had sent them back. He apologized for not being able to send us back because of a shortage of equipment. I talked to the other two guys, and we became turret gunners in the armoured cars until we returned to their base. I had to hide a laugh because they said they were on a recon and this happened to be their target. He explained that some of the armoured cars didn't even have gunners. When I was taken prisoner, the sergeant and I were on a recon. Alone. I figured they had five Jeeps with all the Brownings mounted, at least five tanks and half a dozen armoured cars. And they were under strength?

Perhaps they had lost some men when we first heard the shooting. One of the fellows told me the action was a roadblock with a machine gun nest manned by women. He had tears in his eyes as he told me. "We had to wipe them out. They wouldn't quit and we had to wipe them out." He shook his head and walked away. I felt sorry for him. It sure shook him up. At that time, I'm afraid my feelings were not as tender as his. But then again, I never had to shoot up a machine gun nest full of women.

Later on, we met up with the other four escapees. Big reunion! When we met the American army, we felt euphoria. We had done it! We made it! I was on cloud nine. I was also very proud to know I had helped. And I am sure someone was looking after us, for we managed to get the seven of us out to the free world. If we hadn't turned down that road, if the three young soldiers were not there, if we had just missed the patrol, because that is what it was. Someone had to be guiding us.

They wanted to ship us in open trucks. I asked for a closed truck or a van. As the spokesman for the group, I explained that our health wasn't the best. We would probably all catch colds, if not worse, and with respect, requested even if we had to wait for it, something closed in. The transport sergeant told the captain that they had three civilian cars now. How about a couple of them? So we got them. One was an Opel. It looked just like the 1940 Chevy we had back home, it was even the same blue shade. The other may have been a Ford. They said follow the convoy back. "By the way, can you drive?" the sergeant asked. Three of us said we could. The Americans gassed them up. "The convoy will lead you, so you can get back to England."

Well, we followed them to the first Y in the

road; they went right and we went left. We figured if we could sell the two cars, we could see Paris before going home. We could have a ball. This was a great idea, except for MPs and bridges. The first bridge we came to, we ran into an MP. He said: "Just where do you boys think you're going?" We said we'd had enough of the war and we were going home. Now an MP's sense of humour is no better than that of little German coal miners. He said, "Oh, you are, are you? Well, just turn around and pull in over there, boys."

We explained where we got the cars, but it did no good. He kept pointing to the parking lot. We parked the cars, went into the building where we explained our presence. We found these people quite human. This was a small hotel that had also been taken over by the military. They gave us rooms. We bathed. They gave us a British uniform, underwear, sock, boots and shaving gear. We slept in the hotel beds, and in the morning after *break-fast*, we were taken to an airport.

The driver told us President Roosevelt had died. That knocked us for a loop. I felt very bad about that. He was a good President in a time when the Americans needed one. If he had lived a little longer, he could have seen the end of the war, at least in Europe.

11

Safe At Last

OUR PLANE CAME IN, and we got on board and sat on bench seats on either side of the plane. It was Friday the thirteenth. I noticed a parachute hanging next to what looked like a urinal and I thought, "If I hear a sputter from one of the engines, I'll have that on as fast as I can."

Soon the pilot called out that he was going to bank the plane and for us to look out the right side windows. We flew low, and we could see the white cliffs of Dover. In a short time we were in England. We went to Aldershot where the army billeted us but didn't know what to do with us, as we were the first group of ex-POWs. They gave us a medical and weighed us. I had gained and now I was a hundred and ten pounds. The doctor said it wasn't uncommon to gain a pound a day in my condition. They told us the dining room in the mess hall was open to us at any time. They said eat whatever we felt like, but not too much at a time.

The next group of POWs they put in the hospital. I guess we got them to thinking about what was to be done.

We were told we could go on leave if we wanted to. For once, I had money to do this without pinching pennies. I had twenty-four-months back pay. The problem was I was too weak to do much. I mostly sat back and watched. I visited my aunt and uncles in Whitley Bay in the north of England. I didn't do much; I sat around and rested, returned to Aldershot and waited.

We were free to do just about anything we wanted. We had the run of the camp. The war ended one day when we were in a camp movie. A typed message was slipped onto the screen, and the movie continued. After the show, someone said, "Let's go to London." So away we went. I stood back and watched the crowds. It was great to see everyone so happy. Britain had been through so much.

In London, I walked past a group of Army girls. When I heard them, I knew they were Canadian. It was so nice to hear Canadian girls' voices again. People would stop me and ask if I was all right, or if they could help me. I guess I really looked sick, and I was a walking skeleton. The salt from the mine had bleached me so white that I guess I looked like death warmed over. Try as I may, I couldn't get a tan that year. I lay in the sun every chance I got, because I didn't want my folks to see me like that. But it was no use. I could not tan.

In a few weeks, we were sent back to Canada. We crossed the Atlantic on the SS *Ile de France*. We slept with the other ranks but ate in the officers' mess on the boat.

We landed in New York City. The Canadians had to wait until the Americans disembarked and were bussed to Grand Central Station. Our driver asked if we had been in New York before. We all said no, so he gave us a tour. About three in the morning, we landed at the station and waited for our train. The Red Cross ladies were there, handing out coffee and donuts. I heard one lady say to another, "See those boys with the red patches on their shoulders? They have been overseas for five years." The other said "My God!" Of course, this wasn't quite true. The Division had been over for five years, but the actual fighting end of the Division? It was not five years.

We boarded our train and started the long trip home to Vancouver. The rest of the fellows had to double up in a bunk, and I, along with the six other POWs, got a lower bunk all to ourselves. The bottom bunks had more room. I felt guilty, so I gave my bunk to the two above me and I took theirs.

For anyone who thinks this country is big, you should try to come home after serving overseas. I thought we would never reach Vancouver. Hope to Vancouver was the longest stretch. I felt I could have walked quicker, but I was just impatient. I washed my face and hands four or five times to clean the soot from the engine off. Maybe I should have left it on. At least it would have given me some colour. We reached Vancouver and had been paid on the train. My turn came to leave the train. I had my pack on and my kit bag, but I had to drag the kit bag because I didn't have the strength to carry it. At the top of the stairs, someone asked me my name. I told him and he announced it over the speaker. I heard a yell and cheers. I rounded the corner and there was the whole family, old friends and neighbours.

I had made it, and I don't know how because I had come so close so many times. I had malaria. I had been shot at by snipers, and an 88 mm gun. I was pelted with three potato mashers (hand grenades). I was shot at with machine gun nine different times, sometimes three at a time. I know they were shooting at me because I was the only one around. The only one that drew blood was the 88 mm. Shrapnel hit me in the left calf, and I had a burn on the inside of my left arm from one of the machine guns.

But I was home and safe at last.

Epilogue

IN APRIL 2003 my wife Paula and I had a visit
from an old neighbour, Lawrie, and her daughter and grandson, aged 12, a nice boy. The lady
that tends our lawn and garden commented that
it was her twentieth anniversary. After she left, I
mentioned I had an anniversary coming up, too.
Lawrie's daughter asked what anniversary it was.
I said, "It will be fifty-eight years since I escaped
from the POW camp where I worked in the salt
mine." I really don't know if Laurie's daughter was
as interested as she seemed or if she wanted her
son Spencer to hear the story. She asked questions,
then said, "Will you tell the story of your escape?"

I told the story beginning with the plan to kick
the ball into the bush. Those of us that were incar-
cerated for sometime under those conditions, I
believe, value freedom a little more than the average person. There are few who can even imagine

the feeling we had even when we were travelling and had no one looking over us. We felt free.

I was amazed when at the end she asked why I risked my life running across an open field to stop the Americans. I couldn't explain that this was the way we did things. After all, we were still in the army. I couldn't stand by and watch a bunch of men die if I could stop it.

By the way, those machine gunners were pretty good. The dirt was being churned up, and they snapped by my ears. That's close! But it's hard to hit a skeleton.

Index

Also from Madrona Books

In Veronica's Garden:
THE SOCIAL HISTORY OF THE
MILNER GARDENS AND WOODLAND
by Margaret Cadwaladr.

The book traces the life of a British aristocrat
who developed significant gardens in Ireland
and Canada. The book was a finalist for
an international award as an outstanding
contribution to the literature of
botany or horticulture.

ISBN 0-9730096-1-6
$34.95 plus GST (in Canada), shipping and handling.

Call 1-800- 866-5504 or e-mail
inveronicasgarden@shaw.ca
to order.